Quackers:

A Writing Strategy
to Improve
Creative Writing
and
Standardized Test Scores

By
Vickie Jo Milleson
and
Emily K. Milleson, Ed.D.

Illustrations By
Connie Jean Keaton

Headline Books, Inc.
Terra Alta, WV

Quackers

To order additional copies of this book
for book publishing information,
or to contact the author:

Headline Kids
 P. O. Box 52
Terra Alta, WV 26764
www.headlinekids.com

Tel/Fax: 800-570-5951
Email: mybook@headlinebooks.com
www.headlinebooks.com
www.headlinekids.com

ISBN 0-929915-89-5
ISBN-13: 978-0-929915-89-0

Library of Congress Cataloging-in-Publication Data

Milleson, Vickie Jo.
  Quackers : a writing strategy to improve creative writing and standardized test scores / by Vickie Jo Milleson and Emily K. Milleson ; illustrations by Connie Jean Keaton.
     p. cm.
  ISBN 978-0-929915-89-0
  1. Creative writing--Study and teaching. 2. English language--Composition and exercises. 3. Educational tests and measurements--United States--Interpretation. 4. Examinations--United States--Interpretation. I. Milleson, Emily K. II. Keaton, Connie Jean. III. Title.
  PE1404.M555 2011
  372.62'3044--dc22
                              2010052957

PRINTED IN THE UNITED STATES OF AMERICA

Dedication

To
Mrs. Louisa Miller Hardy

A gracious lady, and the wonderful teacher
who taught me how to write,
V. J. M.

To
My mother,
Jill R. Parker

Who was my first teacher,
E. K. M.

To
Ralph C. Keaton

A caring teacher
who inspired many students,
C. J. K.

Foreword

Like many teachers in West Virginia, when we first learned that the state would be changing to the **WESTEST** as our annual standardized assessment, I was immediately concerned as to how my students would perform on this new testing format. Up until this point, all I had to worry about was teaching the "facts." Students simply took a multiple choice test. All that was seen on that test was a blackened dot made by the student. Nothing else about that student was revealed on paper.

Now teachers were being told that the students would not only have to answer multiple choice questions, but they would also have to write! The writing is what worried me. I felt vulnerable! Remember, up until now, all that was shown about the student was that black dot. If the student missed the question, it was just a reflection on the student that he or she did not know or remember that particular fact.

Please do not "get me wrong." I had always worked hard to have high tests scores, but now I simply felt more pressure for my students to perform well on standardized testing. Not only would the facts I taught be tested, but also, all of the different components that go into producing good writing would be tested as well. For the first time, I felt my teaching was truly being exposed for severe scrutiny. In other words, "I got scared!"

Along with getting the facts to the questions correct, how would my students ever remember all of the components that go into producing good writing? Over the next few months before testing time, I surely asked myself this question hundreds of times. One word, though, always continued in my thoughts: organization. I had to have my students organized; I had to have an easy way for them to remember all of the important components to good writing.

As often happens, I stumbled upon the answer quite by accident. Becoming exasperated with my students one day while I was teaching (can you imagine that?!!), I simply said, "You must get your ducks in a row."

From that point, **Quackers** was born. She and her little ducklings became my students' rubric.

Introduction

As I stated in the title of this book, **Quackers** is not a writing program. It is a strategy I use to prepare my students for standardized testing. In my case, it is preparation for the **WESTEST 2**. Consequently, I do not begin this strategy the first day of school, the first month of school, and sometimes, not even the first semester of school. When I feel my students know enough of the components that go into good writing, I feel they are ready for **Quackers**.

Now a good question at this point would be, what do I think are the components of good writing? I believe the students should have a working knowledge of the following skills:

1. Basic knowledge, appropriate for the grade level, of how to write a paragraph:
   a. To indent a two-finger space
   b. To write a good topic sentence
   c. To know to write at least two to three (or more, depending upon grade level) detail sentences in a paragraph

2. Basic knowledge, appropriate for the grade level, of punctuation:
   a. To begin a sentence, proper nouns, proper adjectives, and all important words with a capital letter (This may sound extremely basic, but it is unbelievable the number of students who fail to do this, regardless of the grade level.)
   b. To use commas correctly
   c. To use quotation marks correctly
   d. To use end punctuation marks correctly

3. Basic knowledge, appropriate for the grade level, of:
   a. Parts of speech
   b. Figures of speech

4. A basic understanding that writing can serve as a means to communicate thoughts and stories with others:
   a. To make stories through writing
   b. To use writing to make the imagined concrete
   c. To view writing as owned by the writer and as a reflection of self
   d. To try out other perspectives and experiences through writing.

5. Finally, my own personal favorite, depending upon the grade level, is good manuscript or cursive handwriting skills.

One might now think, if my students can do all of this, they do not need a writing strategy to help them. Unfortunately, not all of our students can do all of this, and those that can, all too often, forget. At this point, when students are struggling and forgetting, **Quackers** comes to the rescue. Remember, all of these components on how to write have been introduced to the students. We will reteach and review these skills as we do **Quackers,** and it will be fun!

Please remember, though, that **Quackers** is a strategy of my own imagination. I certainly do not consider myself an expert or the final authority in writing. The following are simply ideas and strategies that have worked exceptionally well over the years for me. I might add, though, after hearing about my **Quackers** strategy, I had a high school teacher tell me she adapted it effectively for her English classes.

By the way, Chapter 10, has absolutely nothing in the world to do with **Quackers**. I added this chapter because I thought perhaps some of these activities I do in the classroom might be helpful to other teachers.

In the following pages, I will begin each chapter with my strategies and ideas for use in the classroom. When the text appears in a different format, those are the comments of Dr. Emily Milleson. Her comments provide a research-based context for the strategy.

V. J. M.

Table of Contents

NOTES:

- Teachers are entertainers
- Ducks are in a row like the writing process
- trying to draw "bad" ducks are more so enjoyed by the students ...

Chapter One

Quackers

The first time I ever introduced **Quackers** to my students I simply walked to the front of my classroom and drew a picture of a large duck on the chalkboard. The sketch immediately had the students laughing because, first, my lack of artistic skills, and secondly, the simple fact that I had drawn a duck on the board. I had their attention. They were curious to know what that silly duck had to do with what I was getting ready to teach.

In any situation, the effective teacher must first have the attention of her students. Current classroom teachers have a harder job of this than ever before in the history of education. Students are accustomed to being entertained. Whereas, in the past, children played with toys that used their imaginations, now students sit in front of a screen and expect entertainment. We teachers are not only educators now, but in a way, have also assumed the role of entertainers. My first thought in using **Quackers** was, this is great entertainment! Now, if I can just keep the class with me…

I explained to the class that this mother duck was named **Quackers** (more laughter) and that she was going to help us with our writing skills. I asked the students if any of them knew how baby ducklings followed their mother. Eventually someone said, or perhaps I led them to say, "in a row." This was the cue I wanted from the students. I then told them being organized and getting "our ducks in a row" was important in our writing.

Since that first introduction of **Quackers**, I have become a little more "polished" in my presentation. I have purchased colorful mother duck and duckling cutouts from various teacher supply houses. (Although I have not yet tried this with my new electronic board in my classroom, I feel certain ducks could be found from a media source to use as models for the strategy.) I have the purchased ducks laminated and use them year after year. Magnetic clips attach the ducks to my chalkboard. These ducks are colorful and cute, but I must admit, I think the children still prefer my silly drawings!

My theory on drawing my own ducks is students like to see that we, as teachers, are also not perfect. It gives the children the opportunity to laugh at me! They see I cannot draw and know you can still be smart and not do **all** things really well. Consequently, I always draw my own ducks at some point during the course of teaching **Quackers.**

Emily's Perspective:

In introducing **Quackers** to students, it is important to develop memorable writing cues and an overall atmosphere for writing in the classroom. When addressing the topic of writing instruction, it is critical to create an environment where students are empowered to make mistakes as writers. All too often, students are intimidated by the writing task, as writing makes their thinking visible and permanent. An incorrect thought (or one that is perceived to be incorrect by the student) does not bear as much weight, visibility, and potential embarrassment as putting that "wrong" answer into writing. By showing learners that writing is a process, with clear and simple rules for success and room for error alongside growth, we allow students to overcome their trepidation and take pencil in hand.

Additionally, the cute ducklings in this strategy make the components of writing less intimidating. They serve as visible reminders of the critical elements in good writing while also communicating that writing is fun! When the "rules" of writing are paired with instruction that is entertaining and approachable, writing itself becomes an enjoyable affair.

Chapter Two

The Ducklings

Once I have introduced **Quackers**, the mother duck, to the students, I then introduce her various ducklings. I have introduced them in two different ways, depending upon my class.

My preferred method is to guide the students to give me the answers that I want from them. I start by asking the students what is important in good writing. For each relative response received from a student, we make up a nickname from that response for a duckling. For example, if a student said good punctuation was important, we might name a duckling, "Punky."

I then draw a duckling behind the mother duck on the chalkboard. I write the name we have given the duckling either on or above it. If I am using the laminated ducklings, I use a small magnetic clip and put the duckling following **Quackers**. Because the duckling is laminated, I use erasable markers and write on the duckling, or simply use chalk and write the name of the duckling above it on the chalkboard.

If I have a class that is not quite as creative, I name the various ducklings myself. I usually try to limit the ducklings to seven. If I have too many ducklings, the students will be on overload. Overwhelming the students will defeat my purpose of remembering the components of good writing.

Once the class has named the ducklings for the various components of good writing, we will use those names for the remainder of the school year. Reminder: this is a strategy to help students **remember** those various writing components. Changing the names of the ducklings defeats our purpose of remembering them!

This is the part which the students absolutely love! After I have introduced the ducklings, and the students are writing, I walk around the classroom spot-checking their work. (Nothing unusual about that, you are thinking.) As I walk by a student's desk, though, if I see a mistake of any kind, I point my finger at the mistake and "quack!" That's right, I "quack." I "quack" according to the mistake. If it is just a little mistake, I give a little "quack." If it is a major mistake that the student should not have made, I will go "quack, quack, quack…" So, eventually, the student knows the seriousness of his/her mistake according to my "quacks!"

I realize not all teachers may choose to "quack." Some of us just do not have that type of personality. In fact, some classes may not do well with the quacking. If either of these be the case, I would simply walk around the classroom monitoring the students' work.

If you can, though, quacking really does work. An extra benefit I have found from the "quacking" is that it helps the students who are at a lower developmental level in writing. They may be the ones who make the most mistakes; they may be the ones who get the most "quacks." Since the students love to hear me "quack," the students who are struggling writers receive a great deal of attention. They are the ones who are making me "quack." Instead of receiving negative attention, though, everyone is laughing and having fun! In fact, there have been a few times when I felt mistakes were made on purpose by some of my higher achieving students just to hear me "quack!"

In the following chapters, I will be giving you the ducklings that I name and use with **Quackers**. I will also be sharing with you my "helpful hints" or "tricks" for scoring well on the writing segment of standardized tests. (Students love secrets, so I usually tell them my "tricks" are a secret, and they are to tell no one!)

I truly believe there are certain things all students, **regardless of their developmental level**, can do, and it will **definitely** improve their writing scores! I have seen these improvements happen with my own students, including those in special education classes. Also, a great by-product of these "tricks" is that they not only improve writing scores on standardized tests but in writing in general!

Emily's Perspective

For reluctant writers, the written word can seem to be a "code" that requires "tricks" and "hints" in order to be used effectively. Through **Quackers**, the critical elements of writing are provided under the guise of revealing secrets; in doing so, we are helping our students break the "code" of writing. After learning what each duck represents, young writers can experience ownership of the writing craft and use the "code" of the written word to better communicate their personal experiences and their understandings regarding content.

The use of humor in the naming of the ducks and through the "quacking" reminders can also add to the approachability of writing tasks. When students are gently reminded of mistakes by using the ducklings, we are also communicating a powerful message: writing is a process filled with errors along the way. The goal of the program is not to have students writing perfect papers on the first try, but to equip learners with the critical tools of the writing process. (See Appendix A for an illustration of **Quackers** relationship to the writing process.) Addressing writing from this standpoint allows students to see the value in their **growth** as writers, in addition to the writing pieces that they produce.

NOTES:

- important for good writing?
  - punctuation → Punky the duck

Quackers   Punky
"Mom"

- walk around room to analyze
  writing - small mistake → "quack"
        - big mistake → "quack" "quack"
                "quack"

Chapter Three

Indy, Spacey, or Space Cadet

I call this little duck Indy, Spacey, or Space Cadet. He is extremely important on a standardized test. This is especially true for your struggling writers. As if you have not already guessed, this little duckling is all about spacing. Choose your favorite name!

In any situation, I am a firm believer in first impressions, whether it be meeting someone for the first time or buying a product. I firmly believe we are influenced by our very first thoughts in any given situation. So it is with our writing.

Spacing plays a very important role in the overall appearance of our writing. Before we even read one word of a paper, we judge that paper by how it looks. Writing that is neatly spaced not only gives the appearance of neatness, but may even give the appearance of more writing, and, thus, more knowledge.

When practicing for the writing segment of a standardized test, I tell my students it is very important to look at the space that has been given to them in which to write. If they have been given one, two, or three blank pages for any type of written response, **never** start writing on the top line. Why? That is a great many pages for a student to complete. We want to **take up space!** My students hear those three words over and over again as we practice our writing. The only time I recommend starting on the top line of any written response is when the student feels space is limited. Then, I recommend he/she start writing on the top line.

I suggest to the students they come down at least two spaces on their paper and then, always, write a title. Why? Not only is a title a necessity in some writing, it makes all writing look more polished and professional. Another reason, you got it, a title takes up space!

Everyone loves a great and clever title. I tell the students it is the title which really first "grabs" the reader's attention. So, good titles are important. Unfortunately, we cannot always think of one; especially when you are ten years old, taking a standardized test, and being clever is a constant difficulty.

When we are in this situation, I just tell the students not to worry about the title. Use a title, but do not spend a great deal of time worrying about the title. If worse comes to worse, just give the judges back what they have asked you for in your writing. If you are asked to describe the Statue of Liberty, let that be your title. I tell my students sometimes it is just better to have a title than it is to worry about being clever. Watch: your struggling writers will smile at this statement and be visibly relieved. This is what you want for them: to relax and do their very best in their writing!

After writing the title, I tell the students they need to skip a space. It looks nice. It also takes up space! Often, though, if a student cannot immediately think of a title, I tell them it is all right to wait until their paper is finished. Sometimes, it is easier to think of a title when a paper is completed.

This next statement may seem ridiculously simple, but it is very important in writing. Students must begin a new paragraph every time the subject changes in their writing. These paragraphs **must** be indented. If the students are taking the test online, I tell them to tap the space bar five times or use the tab key. If we are writing by hand, I have my students use the primary method of "two finger indent."

I have students in the fifth grade who do not indent. Telling the students this is the correct grammatical way of writing does not impress them. They have been given this reason since the first grade! I use another reason to indent, and the students do not forget this one. Indenting takes up space! Students realize this is space in which they do not have to write. Trust me, they **will not** forget this reason. It works! Students will not forget to indent because it means less work for them!

I also always have the students skip a space between paragraphs. It makes their writing look neater. The other reason, you got it, it takes up space. Here is another helpful hint I give my students on "using up" space. When space allows, always write the question back into the answer. It not only takes up space, but there are two added benefits. One, it keeps the student focused on his/her writing, and two, it makes the opening sentence sound impressive and intelligent.

Of course, these hints are for taking up space and for making student writing look nice. These hints will not guarantee good writing content, but it will give a good first impression, and that should count for at least one point!

Two years ago, for the first time, we received news that our county would be taking the writing assessment portion of our standardized test, the **WESTEST 2**, online. I must admit that I really worried that perhaps my **Quackers** strategy might not be of any use to me since we would be using the computer. I need not have worried.

About a month before testing time, I had my students use the state online writing practice program for the **WESTEST 2**. I was able to access the program online and assign different types of writing prompts to my class. Students would log into the program and read their prompt. On paper I would have them do their prewrite and rough draft, then log back into the program to type. The program would automatically format their writing; the spacing, indenting, etc., was done for them. Also, if they typed a poor sentence or a misspelled word, these would appear in a different color to alert the student of a mistake. All the student had to do was fill in the beginning, middle, and end sections of the program.

What most teachers absolutely love about the program is that upon finishing the student may simply submit their paper online, and it is instantly graded. The rubric used for grading explains what is correct or incorrect with the writing. The student may then generate a hard copy of his/her writing. The paper is finished, graded and ready for his/her creative writing folder. Sounds great, doesn't it? Remember the old adage, "if it sounds too good to be true, it probably is?" I found this to be partly true with the program.

By the time my students got to the computer lab to practice for their online writing assessment, I had taught the **Quackers** strategy. My students already knew the importance of neatness, spelling, grammar, spacing, etc. My first thought was that perhaps I had wasted my time; spacing, for example, was going to be done for them. I had forgotten for a moment the first rule I was taught concerning computers: computers are only as smart as the person using them. Students still need to know the rules of grammar. We all know spell check does not always work; homophones are a good example. Grammar check is the same. I was so glad my students knew their grammar because when a sentence came up a different color, they could usually figure out the problem.

Also, the first week I used the online writing program I thought perhaps it was broken. Why? All of my students were receiving great scores. No one had received a bad score. I read some of the papers, and I did not think they were so great. I learned something. The online computer grading program standards were not nearly as high as my own. I will not lower my standards; I will continue to teach my **Quackers** strategy, and then I will go to the online practice. The program helps with the students' typing skills, it gets them familiar with writing online, and the feedback builds confidence.

Computers are good. Teachers are good. The combination of the two can be amazing. The student really benefits from both the teacher and the computer. Teach your students first, then, take them to the computer lab for reinforcement! In all my years as a teacher, I have not found a "quick fix" to replace teaching a child. Computers were not put in the schools to replace the teachers. Computers were put in the school as a <u>tool</u> to aid students in learning. Do not think a computer will replace your teaching. Remember, when that happens, we will be out of a job!

I assumed the **WESTEST 2** writing assessment online would be just like the state's online practice program. I was wrong. The students were just given a blank screen. They had to do all the formatting themselves. **Quackers** came to their rescue! The students did not hesitate, and I was pleased with the results.

This year we have a new state online writing assessment practice program. I have only had time to use it twice, but I can say this: although the format is the same, this program grades much harder than the previous one. I am only just learning the program, but I have quickly noticed several ways to improve scores. The program does not like pronouns. I have found that students do better when they simply rename their subjects. The program also likes lots of words, especially words with more than one syllable. Additionally, be careful with people's names. The program wants to count older spellings of names and different spellings of names as incorrect. For example: my students each wrote on someone famous from the period of the American Revolution. Almost every name used from that period was underlined as misspelled. I am sure as the year progresses, I will learn even more about the program.

Emily's Perspective

To truly understand the importance of teaching students the rules of formatting in written language, I find that it is helpful to draw a comparison between speaking and writing. When students have limited experiences with formal speaking, teachers must provide direct instruction about the norms for spoken communication, and often will establish rules for addressing adults, and for sharing information in class. These teachers are providing students the guidelines for speaking in school and in turn, most learners adjust their language to meet these expectations.

In its most casual form, writing is simply a way to communicate between individuals; think of the scribbled note being passed between friends, or the text message sent from one cell phone to another. However, writing also requires a formal tone when it is being used as a means for the demonstration of understanding. This is the case with many written assignments in the classroom, and the case with most standardized testing. Direct instruction, regarding formatting, is especially important in our current era where technology usage for personal communication has softened our adherence to the rules of grammar.

Just as we prepare students to use the correct speech in an interview, we must prepare students to use the formalities of writing. Guidelines for indention, spacing, and grammar can be viewed as the etiquette of the written word, a gesture of politeness extended to the reader. By following the established guidelines for formal writing, the student has the advantage of communicating in a manner that matches the expectations for a written exam. When the piece of writing created is a reflection of the norms for formatting, the writer has shown himself/herself to be demonstrating the correct level of written communication. Additionally, the time spent on the presentation of the written word transfers to appeal for the reader.

 *NOTES:*

Chapter Four

Comma Queen and Cap
Goody I and Goody II
The Little Match Duck

The Comma Queen, Cap, Goody I and Goody II, and The Little Match Duck are all favorite names of mine I have used for the ducklings over the years. As I have stated before, the ducklings may be named anything you feel is important for your students to remember. I just wanted to share with you the reasoning behind these names.

Comma Queen and Cap are really not necessary when you use the duckling, Punky, because he stands for punctuation. I use them anyway. It is a personal thing!

The Comma Queen is me! I tell my students the rule of thumb when it comes to commas is "when in doubt, leave it out." I do not listen to this rule; I absolutely love commas! (It is very obvious in my books. My husband would say it is my "flair for the dramatic!" I always feel commas and exclamation points help me to "emphasize" what I have to say!)

The students think this is so funny I do not follow a rule which I know to be correct. (The other rule I love to "break" is beginning a sentence with a conjunction!) I tell them this is a time (probably, of many!) when they **should not** follow my example, and, you know, it works! When I review their writing with them, they always laugh when I start putting in commas. They say the Comma Queen is at work. They actually will argue with me that a comma is not needed in a certain place. I love it! The students are learning to correct the teacher! Sometimes, I just have to give in to the students because I really cannot justify the comma. When I draw the Comma Queen on the chalkboard, I always put a crown on her head. When I use the laminated ducklings, I still draw a crown between her head and her name. I guess this is as close as I will ever get to royalty…

Cap is a snappy little duckling who stands for capitalization. Besides the first word of a sentence, proper nouns, and proper adjectives, there are other words students must remember to capitalize. Titles, which I feel are very important on the writing segment of any standardized test, need to be capitalized. Once again, I tell students they need to remember the rule of thumb, "capitalize the first word, the last word, and all important words in between," when writing a title.

Goody I and Goody II are extremely important little ducklings. Once again I have one of my famous "secrets" to share with the students. As usual, this secret is told as a hyperbole—an extreme exaggeration! (I do love those figures of speech; we not only learn their meanings and how to use them, we learn how to spell all the figures of speech!)

I tell the students their first job as a writer is to literally "grab the attention" of their reader. The main goal of any writer is to have their writing read. When taking a standardized test, the student needs to grab the attention of the judges. So, give me a good beginning, thus Goody I. Emphasize the good beginning over and over to the students. They must latch on to the judge or reader, and they must keep them reading!

Goody II refers to the end of a student's writing. They must give the reader a good ending to remember. When I say good, I do not mean it in the sense of always a "happy" ending. I mean good as in a well-written ending. Consequently, I tell the students my "big" secret. Give the judge or reader a good, strong beginning and a good, strong ending, and the judge or reader will probably "forgive you a little, if you get lost in the middle." (Yes, I made that up, too!) Goody I and Goody II will also take some pressure off your struggling writers who worry that all parts of their writing "must be perfect" for them to "pass the test."

Finally, we come to The Little Match Duck. This is another duckling that is especially important to our developing writers. As I stated in the previous paragraph, a good ending is a must in all writing. Sometimes, though, it is difficult to be clever. Here is where The Little Match Duck comes to our rescue.

Just give the judges back what they have asked you for in their own question. This is great! We do not even have to think. Tell the students they only have to match their last sentence to their first sentence, and they are finished with a good ending! For example, if the students are asked to write about a day at the beach, their last sentence could simply read, "This was my wonderful (or terrible, whatever the case may be) day at the beach." It is a good ending sentence that reminds the reader what the writing was all about in the first place.

One final word of advice I give my students on endings is how **not** to end their writing. Never conclude with

The End!

Emily's Perspective

In considering Little Match Duck, Goody I and Goody II, I am reminded of the importance of having direction in writing. By emphasizing the drafting phases of the writing process, and helping students to identify the starting and ending points of their writing, teachers can aid developing writers in the creation of complete writing pieces. Often, student writing seems to drop off at the end of a composition, as students are unsure about how to bring their writing to a close. By tying the title and the closure together, students are given the confidence of knowing where their writing is headed, and the reassurance that a good beginning will serve them well when they are finishing up their thoughts. As a reader, it is often this "sandwich" approach that motivates me to continue a book. I am always excited when a piece of information that I noticed at the start of a novel ends up being critical in a latter part of the text.

The ducks in this chapter also emphasize the importance of cementing key points for the reader. As students are reminded of the "judges" who evaluate writing on standardized assessments, we can also make them critical readers of their own work by placing them in the position of a "judge." For example, students are reminded that quality in writing is what keeps the intended audience reading. An awareness of what makes individuals want to begin a book, keep reading a book, and most importantly, recommend a book to someone else, can serve students as writers. By emphasizing the demands of an audience, students will transfer their expectations for good writing into their own compositions.

 *NOTES:*

Chapter Five

Neatness and Handwriting

I must be honest. Of all the ducklings, Neat Nick is my own personal favorite. He was the very first duckling I named. Due to my love of alliteration, this duckling was named the year I had Nick in my fifth grade class.

The reason I mention Nick is because I often name the ducklings after a student. This is especially true if I can use alliteration. I have found students really enjoy having a duckling named for them. Thus, again, the names of the ducklings may change year after year, at your discretion. Also, it reinforces the figure of speech, alliteration.

Neat Nick has to do with both manuscript and cursive handwriting. As I stated before in my chapter on spacing, I am a firm believer in first impressions. Finally, students with good handwriting can shine and receive credit for it!

Let me use Tim (name has been changed) as an example. Years ago Tim was a student of mine who had been "written out" of the special education program. When he entered my classroom, he had never passed a standardized test in his life—in any subject. I saw, though, that Tim had great potential in cursive handwriting. This is where I started working with Tim. We had to find **something** in which he could succeed in order for him to be successful in his academic work. (I am also a firm believer in the old adage, "nothing succeeds like success!") It worked! Tim became one of the neatest students in my classroom.

When we began practicing for the writing assessment, I asked my students what would be the first thing the judges would see of our creative writing. Immediately, they answered, our cursive handwriting. This is when I made what I call my "big statement." I told the class even if Tim wrote zebras had circles, instead of stripes, he would receive some kind of credit on his test. Why? Tim's handwriting was so incredibly neat, the judges were going to be impressed. Tim would get a point on his handwriting alone. Every time I said this, Tim beamed. Consequently, Tim "fell in love" with creative writing. He felt he was going to receive something for his effort. And you know what—he became a very good writer. Why? If we believe we are good at something, regardless of whether we are or not, that belief will carry us through to succeed. Tim did! That year, for the first time, Tim achieved "mastery" on all parts of the **WESTEST**!

Good writing, manuscript or cursive, is so rare, when judges see beautiful handwriting that alone impresses them. When your struggling writers use the **Quackers** spacing tricks and good handwriting, they are going to be helped on standardized tests. These strategies will also carry over to all writing in any subject.

In our county, cursive handwriting is mandatory for students in grades three through twelve. Consequently, only cursive handwriting is acceptable in my classroom, period. However, I do have students who enter my fifth grade classroom unable to write in cursive. (We find these are mostly students who enter our school from other counties or states.) Unless the child cannot write due to a developmental or physical limitation, they leave my classroom writing in cursive. It is what is expected of me as a teacher. We must take the time and teach these children how to write in cursive. Then, why did I mention manuscript writing? As always, there are exceptions to every rule. This even applies to my rule on complete cursive handwriting.

Graphic organizers are where we use our manuscript skills. Graphic organizers are on standardized tests. This is when manuscript is not only acceptable, but it is the correct handwriting to use. When we do our "lists" (which are graphic organizers) for our writing, we do this in manuscript.

Two things I would like to mention before I leave Neat Nick. First, please do not use the term "sloppy copy" in your classroom. This term makes sloppiness correct. I encourage neatness in our classroom at all times. (This even applies to their desks. I always tell the students when I want to see sloppiness, I will go to a pig pen. When I want to see neatness, I will come to school.) In my classroom, we do a "rough draft." They are the same thing, but the connotation is so much better.

Secondly, please, never punish a student by making them write sentences. Writing one hundred times, "I will not talk in class," destroys good handwriting. Worse, it makes students hate writing of any kind—cursive, manuscript, or creative.

Good cursive handwriting is truly becoming a lost art. Do not let this happen in your classroom. This is a life skill. Everyone appreciates a neatly written thank you note for a birthday, graduation, wedding, baby shower, etc., gift. If a student gives me an apple, or for that matter anything, they receive a handwritten thank you note from me in my very best handwriting. (Yes, if I make a mistake, I do it again.) We must model what we expect of our students. It is our job.

I realize not every student will write the letters of the handwriting chart perfectly—some, not even close. Our job, though, is to make sure each student writes his/her very best. When we accomplish this, then we have accomplished our goal.

Emily's Perspective

Often overlooked in the writing curriculum, instruction in handwriting can be significant when developing writing fluency. Research conducted with first graders, who were developing writers, showed that explicit instruction in handwriting led to gains in overall writing and compositional fluency. (Graham, Harris, and Fink, 2000) This study showed the importance of teaching handwriting skills in the elementary years, as improved handwriting had a direct influence on the overall quality and amount of writing that students produced. Additionally, focusing instructional time on proper letter formation can increase student attitudes about their writing. Celebrating student success in handwriting can positively shape students' self-concepts regarding writing; first the handwriting is celebrated, then students begin to write more and to feel that indeed, they are a "writer."

The importance of neatness in the classroom is an area of instruction that can go beyond the topic of writing to the broader issue of student ownership of the classroom environment and of the academic work that they produce. By emphasizing care and thoughtfulness in each phase of a writing assignment (including the rough drafts), students understand there is value in all of the work that they do. This lesson of ownership can translate to feelings of higher self-worth and increased commitment to learning tasks.

Notes:

Chapter Six

"Lying" and "Copying"

I knew this chapter title would get your attention! It draws the same reaction from my students. Yes, sometimes it is perfectly fine to lie and copy on your standardized writing assessment! Now, before I am arrested, let me explain myself.

As I stated earlier, teachers today often have to become entertainers to get their students' attention. The above statement really works! This is one of those times when I tell the students I have a "secret" to share with them. They love my secrets!

When I am preparing my students for their standardized test in writing, I tell them sometimes they may be asked to write about something which has never happened or does not apply to them. For example, I remember on one **WESTEST** practice test I was giving, the assignment was to, "write about a best friend you have had since kindergarten."

Immediately, several hands went up into the air. One child had not entered public schools until the fourth grade. One child said he had never had a friend (sad, but unfortunately, all too often true.) Several children said they had never had a best friend. Here is how I handle these situations:

I ask the students what kind of test they are taking. They, of course, answer writing. I then ask them if those judges in California really care if they have a friend? (I always say the tests are graded in California because it impresses the students. I do not have a clue where, or by whom, the tests are graded!) After thinking this over, someone will say, no. I then ask the students, what do the judges care and want to know about them? Eventually, they will come up with the answer. The judges want to know if "we can write."

So, I tell the students, lie! Make up a friend! This is great. The student and the fictitious friend (to paraphrase Huckleberry Finn) "can have more fun and more adventures then any two friends could possibly have in a lifetime!" Their writing then will only be limited by their own imaginations. This applies to most all creative writing questions on a standardized test. I tell the students this is wonderful. Here is a test where you can lie and get credit!

Finally, we do calm down, and I do ask the students if they are really lying like we usually think the word means. Of course, they are not. They are being creative on a creative writing test. So, I always stress to my students the fact that whether they have seen the ocean or not, is not important. What is important is whether they can creatively come up with an answer to convince the judges they have seen the ocean. If this means making up something so they can show the people who score the tests they can write, so be it!

Now, let me clarify how it is acceptable to "copy" on a standardized test. Usually, after a writing prompt is given on a standardized test, it says "be sure to include" and lists what a student needs to put in the essay. This is also great! I tell the students they do not even need to think. The test has done it for them. Just give the judges back exactly what they have asked them for on the test and in that order!

For the pre-writing method, I always go with the list, never the web. A web gives you many ideas, but the ideas are not in any type of order. I have found with the web, students will mix up their ideas in the same paragraph.

If the student uses the list method of pre-writing, the ideas are already in paragraph form. The student does not even have to think about which idea goes in which paragraph. The students simply "copy" each item the judges have asked them to include in their essay. Then, they expand on this idea. The student goes to the next item given, and so on. Once the list method is completed, the student writes the essay following the list. I tell the students it does not get any easier than this! Just copy what they ask you to write, and "give it back to them!" Always give it back to the judges in a minimum of three paragraphs with a beginning, a middle, and an end.

Emily's Perspective

Our students come to us with a range of backgrounds, experiences, and writing preferences. Their approaches to writing will differ based on their experiences with language, their home environments, and even their socio-economic backgrounds. For some students, limited background experiences can make writing to prompts an intimidating event; this is especially true for a writer who does not have a personal context or knowledge base for the topic that he/she is being asked to address.

Research by Jane Gradwohl and Gary Schumacher (1989) showed that when student content knowledge was measured for topics that they preferred to write about versus topics they did not want to write about, the students had significantly more knowledge about the preferred topics. Students also demonstrated more content knowledge about preferred writing topics than teacher-selected topics. This research shows the importance of allowing students the opportunity to select writing topics in order to exhibit their understanding of subjects they find to be interesting and motivating. It makes sense that we would all enjoy writing about things that we know well.

This study also shows the importance of creating experiences which build content knowledge for topics students do not know well. As we increase student understanding of a broad range of content, we can also expand the amount of topics they feel comfortable writing about. If students have limited experiences with the writing topics which are prompted from their teacher and/or assessments, we must allow these students opportunities to develop insight regarding these topics. This can be done with the use of quality literature, role-playing, and multi-media experiences. The "cheating" aspect of **Quackers** is a humorous way to teach developing writers how to use their experiences and content knowledge when writing about unfamiliar topics. By emphasizing the directions within the prompts, students are given an approachable strategy for meeting the requirements of this writing activity with success.

 *Notes:*

Chapter Seven

Writing:
It Can Only Make You
Look Good!

This is something I truly, truly believe. I tell my students this all the time. When they take a multiple choice exam or a fill in the blank exam, they only have one chance of getting the answer correct. The answer is either right or wrong. They either receive a point for the correct answer or they do not receive a point, end of story, no questions asked! There is no room for mercy.

For example, the question may ask what great document was authored by Thomas Jefferson. The student may remember many things about Jefferson, but cannot at that moment remember the Declaration of Independence. This "mental block" happens to all of us at one time or another. When it happens on a standardized test, it is really detrimental to the student's score.

This is when I tell the students they can "shine" on the writing portion of a test. On the writing portion of a standardized test, or any test for that matter, we are "allowed" to forget some details. If we can remember enough other details to satisfy the judges that we know something about Thomas Jefferson, or any question asked, we will usually be given some credit for our answer. Granted, we may not receive a perfect score, but it is better than the zero we would have received on the objective test.

Consequently, writing can make students look better. It gives them a chance to share what knowledge they do know about the question with the judges.

 *NOTES:*

Chapter Eight

Writing:
Not Always a Graded
Subject and More

In my classroom, whether we are preparing for standardized testing or not, we are writing. For what they are worth, I would like to share with you some things I do concerning creative writing.

On the first day of school, when the students enter my classroom, along with the textbooks on their desks is a brightly colored file folder, which will be their creative writing folder for the entire year. I explain to the class the purpose of the folder. They are absolutely not to write or draw on it. On the top lip of the folder, they are to very neatly write their complete name in cursive. That is all.

In the past, I had hanging on the wall beside the entrance door to my classroom, a plastic file container. I had the students put their file folders in this container in alphabetical order. This was where their writing folders remained until the end of the school year. At that time, the folders, with their writing, was sent home. The files were also easy to access for anyone who was observing in my classroom or requested to see the students' writing.

I still follow that same procedure, but I had to move the students' files; we were doing so much writing the wall file simply could not hold all their work, besides becoming too heavy for the wall. Now, I have a file box (recycled from a book company sample) on a bookcase under my **Quackers** bulletin board. I ran off on yellow computer paper a sign that says Fifth Grade Creative Writing and pasted it over the book company's name. I also put cute **Quackers** stickers on the label. The box is attractive, useful, handy, and cheap. Students now use this file.

In addition, I would just like to say a few words about my **Quackers** bulletin board. It is a teaching bulletin board that also brightens up my classroom. I have my **Quackers**, mother duck, walking at the head of the line, followed by all her little ducklings. (These are just ducks I purchased and then laminated from a teacher supply company.) At the top of the bulletin board, I have yellow letters cut out spelling **Quackers**. On the bottom of the bulletin board, I have yellow letters cut out saying, "our class writing strategy." This is all bordered in bright yellow on a (this year) hot pink background. Any adult who walks into my classroom always asks me, "What is **Quackers**?" It really grabs the attention of the adults; the children who visit my classroom simply like the cute ducks and bright colors. Of course, my students know what it means, and I have them explain it to our guests. It really is a good way to show off your students and their knowledge of grammar. The guest is always impressed, and the student feels great. What I love best about my **Quackers** bulletin board: it is one bulletin board that I can put up in August and **leave up** all year!!

The bulletin board is also a learning tool because after I have taught the strategy, I do not need to repeat drawing **Quackers** and her ducklings. I simply remind the students to look at the bulletin board and remember to "get their ducks in a row." You can actually see the children sitting there going over the ducklings' names in their heads! It is also a good checklist when they have completed their writing to make sure all the ducklings have been included in their work. Again, this is my students' rubric.

Yes, we do a great deal of writing. Yes, I am the one who reads and corrects all the writing. I am not a fan of letting the students check each other's work in any subject. My theory on this is, if it is important enough for them to do, then it is important enough for me to read. No paper is allowed in their file folder until it is as close to perfect as that student can write. Perfection includes penmanship.

As they finish, each student comes to my desk and, together, we read and correct their work. The student returns to his/her desk to recopy. We repeat the procedure until the writing is completed to our satisfaction. (Yes, sometimes I have to take the papers home with me to correct, but the next day I review the writing with each student and the same procedure continues.)

Grading is where I will differ from most teachers in creative writing. I usually do not put a grade on their creative writing. When the writing is completed to my satisfaction and the student's satisfaction, I put a check on the paper. The student knows a check means the paper is fine. The grammar, spelling, paragraphs, handwriting, etc., are acceptable to my high standards.

Let me explain my "no grade" policy on creative writing. My students are just learning to write. I want to do everything possible to encourage those "creative juices." I cannot do this by putting an "F" on a paper. At their young age, we are modeling and guiding these students a great deal with their writing. With all of this modeling and guiding, I just do not feel justified in putting grades on their work. Frankly, I do not need the grades. Since I collect so many grades in other areas I have the luxury of not needing them. (Our county combines English, reading, spelling, and creative writing grades into one EngLa grade.) I have talked to several reading consultants from major language arts publishing companies about my no grade policy, and they do not have a problem with it. Like me, they feel the important thing is to keep the students writing and wanting to write.

Besides the check, the student also receives a little duck sticker to put on the outside of his/her writing folder. (This is why I tell the students on the first day of school not to write or draw on their folders.) This sticker serves two purposes. One, it is a reward to the student for good work. Secondly, I can tell at a glance how many pieces of creative writing are in a student's folder without taking the time to open each folder. (This also applies to the principal, reading supervisor, or anyone else who would like to see the students' writing.) At a glance, I can tell who has or has not completed each writing assignment, because under each duck I have the student write the name of the assignment, and the date completed.

The stickers also serve as an incentive for the students to write. It is constantly a contest in the classroom to see who has the most duck stickers! You see, every time a student even reads a library book in my class, they must write a report. Since a book report is writing, we follow the same procedures. They write, I check, then they recopy until the report receives a check. That report then receives a sticker. This is where students can really "rack up" the stickers! It is a friendly competition, and really encourages the students to read, which in return, makes the students better writers!

At the end of the school year, my students know I always host a Fifth Grade Reception. This is the time when the students with the most duck stickers are recognized. This recognition is what they have been competing for all year.

By the way, do not think writing a report discourages students to write. We have never failed to meet our class goal of one hundred book reports by Christmas! (I personally check to make sure every student participates in this goal.) To get the students started writing, I make book report forms which I place in a basket in my classroom. After a student has read a book, he or she takes a form. When a student has finished his/her report, he/she puts it in another basket for book reports that I need to check. After I check each report, I return it to the student. The student recopies, and we repeat the procedure until the report receives a check and a sticker.

These book report forms may be changed throughout the year. Of course, the student must always write the title of the book (underlined) and the author's full name. My first form simply has the student to tell me his/her favorite part of the book.

A few notes here: I always (at least in the beginning of the school year) choose the library books for each of my students for several reasons. First, a student may choose books that are simply too hard for his/her reading level. This will quickly turn a student "off" to reading. Secondly, I like to match the reading to what we are studying in class in social studies, etc. Third, I am good at matching a student with a book. Most teachers are good at matching students with books because we know the students, and we know the books. Take the time to help your students find a good book. You will be surprised to see how such little effort on your part, creates more readers in your classroom.

I have read every book my students use for book reports. When I read a book report, I know in a moment whether the book has actually been read! To say I have read all the books my students use for book reports is really no big deal. I love to read, and adults who do not read children's literature are missing some wonderful books!

My "no grade" policy does not extend to most writing across the curriculum assignments. In science and social studies, for example, we are usually not writing "creatively." We are writing for a specific answer. These papers, most definitely, are graded.

Emily's Perspective

When considering whether or not to score a piece of student writing, one must always place high priority on the purpose of the writing activity. In many cases, elementary-aged students are writing to show their thought processes or as a means of creative expression. In these instances, students are also honing their skills as developing writers. This approach, with regards to grading, aligns directly with the goals and purposes for writing in the classroom. **Quackers** is a means to shape student writing development; providing continual feedback and direction for learners without diminishing their motivations to write.

This approach is also consistent with educational theory, demonstrating how to help students improve by working within their "zone of proximal development." This concept, made famous by the work of educational psychologist, Lev Vygotsky, emphasizes the need for students to be presented with work that challenges their learning development, but does not overwhelm them. Teachers provide the challenge and support to allow learners to move forward in small, attainable, but progressively difficult steps.

Student ownership is central to this development and is a key part of the conferencing held with each student regarding his/her writing. Rather than giving students a letter grade with little or no suggestions for improvement, the teacher meets individually with each learner. These conversations help each learner to see the strengths in his/her writing. This empowers all the students to identify areas where they need to make corrections and improvements. The students are not working to please an adult or to meet an arbitrary score; instead, they are growing as individuals and continually making steps towards becoming proficient writers.

The organizational aspects of **Quackers** are important to the successful implementation of the strategy. When students are progressing through the writing process and at times working on multiple writing projects at once, organization of drafts and final pieces is imperative. Keeping final copies in an area where they can easily be seen and read by classroom visitors is also highly motivating for learners, actualizing the idea of writing for a range of audiences. The use of stickers as a reward for learners and as a record-keeping tool allows for accountability, even though most student work does not receive a formal grade.

 *NOTES:*

Chapter Nine

Contests and Publishing

Not only do I call myself the Comma Queen, but also the Queen of the Contests! My goal is to have every student in my class published. I do not care what the academic level is of the student. I want them to leave my classroom as published authors!

There are literally hundreds of creative writing contests for your students to enter throughout the school year. I have my students enter essay, poetry, and short story contests. Trust me, if you enter enough students in enough contests, you, too, will have winners!

It is so exciting to go to your school mailbox and see that special letter from a contest you have entered and know you have a winner! I am as excited as the children to see who has won a prize or is being published!

I always send a letter home to the parents/guardians of my students explaining what I will be doing with their child's writing. The letter serves two purposes: first, it gives me written permission to submit the child's work to publishing companies, and secondly, it serves as another communication between the parents and me. I am keeping the parents aware of what is going on in my classroom. It is such a simple effort on our part as teachers, but one that, I feel, is greatly appreciated by the majority of the parents. (See Appendix B for a sample letter.)

Just a few of the contests I have entered students' writing in over the years, are:
American Legion Essay Contest
Daughters of the American Revolution Essay Contest
Letters About Literature/West Virginia Center for the
Book/West Virginia Humanities Council
Anthology of Poetry Contest

Anthology of Short Stories Contest
Young Poet's Collection Contest
West Virginia Character Counts Essay Contest
D.A.R.E. Essay Contest
…and there are so many more.

They are all free, though some do ask you to supply stamps so they may inform the winners personally at their home address. This is especially true of contests whose winners will not be announced until after school is out for summer vacation. I usually try to avoid those contests. Two years ago, I did enter around seven students in a contest whose results were not announced until the end of July. I made all of the students promise to call me at home if they heard their short stories were going to be published! (I have never had a principal, though, who did not let me submit school postage stamps with these entries. Thus, it still does not cost the students.)

It is wonderful when the students win great, free prizes. For some of my students, it is the first time they have ever won anything. Just imagine what that does for their self-confidence!

Some contests do charge a fee for the book in which a student's work will be published. Regardless of whether the student purchases the book or not, the contests I enter still publish the student's work. Often, many of my parents/guardians buy the books. The students are so proud to bring these books to school to show everyone! (These books do not involve the teacher; the publishing companies deal directly with the parents.)

I tell my students once their work is published, as long as that book exists, so does their writing. When my father published his first book, I remember him telling me that long after he is gone, his book would still be here for people to read. I like to think publishing gives us a touch of immortality. And so it does for our students.

Emily's Perspective

Writing in its purest, simplest form is the communication of our ideas, understandings, and stories. Central to this notion is that the written word is shared. Thus, writing must go somewhere! A student's composition cannot end on the desk of a classroom teacher and be an authentic exercise in writing. It must have an audience and it must be shared with others. This sharing can be as simple as reading a written response aloud to a peer or group of fellow students; it can be the presentation of a poem or play for a classroom of younger learners, or the posting of student writing on a bulletin board in the hallway for a passerby to enjoy.

Having an audience for student writing also allows for the writing itself to be of higher quality. When a learner has a clear picture of who he/she is writing for, he/she is more likely to attend to the details of the written work, adding nuances that best match the expectations of his/her perceived reader. If the only individual reading a student's work is the classroom teacher, we may find the opposite effect occurring. The student begins to narrow his or her writing style to match the expectations of only one reader, the teacher. This can be especially detrimental if a teacher has low expectations or rigid viewpoints regarding writing.

By finding outlets for student work in the community, in competitions, and in publishing, teachers communicate writing has a more realistic and genuine purpose. Students see themselves as "real writers" because their writing is being read by others. Imagine also the sense of pride that comes from seeing one's own writing in print. For developing writers, the acceptance of a piece for publication can be the event that forever changes their perceptions of themselves as writers. Receiving recognition and honor for writing can cement a student's concept of himself/herself as an author.

 *Notes:*

Chapter 10

Something Extra!
Parent and Community Involvement:
It is a Must! Also, Police Involvement!

Several years ago, our county board of education, the county superintendent, or someone in the county, came up with the slogan, (and I am paraphrasing), "it takes a community to educate a child." Since that time, I have come to realize the truth in this statement. Trust me on this: your parents and community can help raise your test scores!

I cannot stress the importance of parent involvement in your classroom. On "Back to School Night," get those parents/guardians on your side! You, as the teacher, the professional, are the one who is going to have to make the first move. It is your job and responsibility, because it **will** benefit your students.

Dwight Morrow, former ambassador to Mexico, and father of Anne Morrow Lindberg, once said (and I paraphrase) that it was always so much easier for him when he first met someone to believe the best in them. I have adopted that philosophy with my parents. When I meet my parents/guardians for the first time, I always tell them I know there is **nothing** in this world they love more than their child. I tell them I take the responsibility of having their child in my classroom seriously, and I will treat their child the way I would want my own children to be treated by a teacher. In fact, I go on to tell my parents their child really is "mine" for the school year since our children are now grown and married! I know this may sound "corny" to some of you, but my parents know I am sincere, and many will respond to me with tears in their eyes. They know I love their child.

Over twenty years ago I came up with another one of my ideas which I still use today, and I think it is a good one. (I must admit, though, for a long time my family did not appreciate this idea!) I gave it my own name and called it my "**positive** phone calls." I try to call my parents/guardians at home every six weeks. I find most of my parents really do want to talk to me about their child and learn what is going on in our class, but they either work, have little ones at home, lack transportation, etc., and cannot make it to school to conference with me. (The reason my husband and, at the time, three teenagers did not like this pre-cell phone idea was because I would tie up the phone line for an evening. Trust me, your family will survive! Now since the children are gone, I always make my calls on Tuesday evenings when my husband has a meeting, and I am the one, "home alone!")

When I make the first call at the beginning of the school year, I explain to the parents/guardians they can expect to hear from me about every six weeks. I will not necessarily be calling with a problem, but rather, I just want to call and let them know what is going on at school and ask if they have any questions concerning school. I also ask their permission to call. My parents really like this idea, and I have **never** had a parent tell me not to call. Yes, I call all the children's parents, even those who have no problems. Those parents also like to hear from the teacher. I tell the parents my calling them is like going to the dentist every six months. We may have a problem, but if we keep in touch, the problem will not become a major one. Like going to the dentist, we will keep our problems small. (It goes without saying, for a major problem a teacher would need to call immediately.)

This next gesture may not work for some of you, but it is not a problem for me. On the first day of school, I have the students write my home phone number in their planners. They or their parents/guardians are free to call me at home if they have any questions or need my help for any reason. I have taught many a parent how to subtract fractions, etc., over the telephone. I appreciate their calling and trying to help their child. In all my years of giving my students my home phone number, my family will agree, I have never had a student or their family bombard me with calls or call me in anger. Besides, our home phone number is in the public directory so I am not even giving out private information about myself; they **have** access to my number. By taking the initiative and giving the parents my number **first**, they seem to feel I am taking an extra step in helping them and their child that is not required of me.

If parents know I am always available to them, it really helps "nip problems in the bud." They know I am not hiding from them. Parents and teachers should never be against each other. We are all on the same team; the team that helps the child. When the student knows the parents and teacher are united, this is a big plus in the classroom. Use your parents! There is no one else who wants your students to succeed as much as them. You **must** keep in contact with your **single greatest resource**!!!

At the beginning of the year, I always explain about my phone calls every six weeks. I tell the students not to be afraid when they hear my voice. I will not be calling to say anything "bad" (always the child's first thought) about them. I am just simply calling to "chat" with their family about school. Frankly, I have found children and their parents love for me to call with good news. Let's face it, when a parent knows a teacher is on the phone, they, like their child, think the worst! Let us change that and make positive phone calls! Incidentally, I tell the children the day I am going to make my calls. This serves several purposes: the children are expecting my call and are not "shocked" when they hear my voice, they will tell me if they will be at a ball game, church, etc., that evening and will not be home until late, or if their parents are working and to call at a certain time. I will also say this about calling: if for some reason I am not able to get through to them that evening, as soon as the student sees me the next day they want to know why I did not call last night! They **want** me to call and brag on them!

Remember, these are always **positive phone calls**. The worst thing I ever say is to remind certain children to study their spelling lists, multiplication facts, etc. If I have to inform parents of something unpleasant, and we all have to sometime, I do it on another phone call. My positive phone calls are to build a good relationship with the students and their families; we cannot do this on "a negative note." I cannot count the times I have asked a mother if she has baked any good holiday cookies or has her shopping finished. With these phone calls, I just "connect" with the family.

Also, in connecting with families, I send what I call "community cards." (I know, I do get carried away with alliteration…) I go to our local dollar stores and stock up on greeting cards at the beginning of the school year. I tell the class if someone in their family is ill, has passed away, needs happy thoughts sent their way, or have a new baby, to tell me, and we as a class will send them a card. Note, community cards are also sent to students within my classroom who are ill, etc. To save myself some money, I do not send many birthday cards (except to my own students), and I do not, as a rule, send the cards through the mail. I let the student who requests the card be the one to deliver it. I have the student tell the name of the person for whom they are requesting a card and the reason they are requesting the card. I draw very pale lines on the cards so when the students sign their names in ink, the names are not slanting, but straight. Before they write their names in cursive, I tell the students if they make a mistake to come to me to fix it—not to mark anything out. I will not let anything leave my classroom unless it is the students' best. I cannot count the number of thank you notes the classes have received over the years for simply sending a card! And everyone **always** comments on their pretty cursive handwriting! Remember, like everything we do, get parent permission first before allowing students to sign their names to greeting cards. (See Appendix C for a sample parent letter.)

A final way I connect with parents is through after-school tutoring. I tutor from two to four students every year after school for three hours a week. I also do summer tutoring. I only tutor my own students during the school year, and I only tutor incoming fifth graders in the summer. Why? Since I am the only fifth grade teacher in our school, I know the fifth grade curriculum better than any other teacher. It only makes sense for me to stay where I am most knowledgeable. I have tutored for free, and I have tutored for pay. (Admittedly, I prefer the latter!) When I am paid, though, it is always through a federal program and **never** by a parent. (Frankly, most of my parents could not afford tutoring.) I keep the children directly after school, and the parents/guardians are responsible for picking up their child following tutoring. This is a good opportunity for me to conference with parents two or three times a week! My parents always seem to appreciate the tutoring, and it is wonderful to work one-on-one with these children and really get to know them. In fact, during the school year, I am usually wait-listed for tutoring!

Community involvement is important to me. In our very small town, I use my limited resources to showcase the talent of my students. I would like to share some of my ideas for community involvement with you.

At the beginning of the school year on "Back to School Night," I give each parent/guardian a packet. I call this packet my "Poetry Contract." In this packet, there is a poem to be memorized for almost each month of school. (I skip the month of March but make up for it with two poems in May. If you are wondering why I skip March, it is just to give the students a break. February is a big month with the memorization of *The Gettysburg Address*.) Also in this packet, is a schedule as to when each poem is due for recitation. Consequently, my students know in August on what days in May they will have a memorized poem to recite. The parents and students know there is no excuse for not having their memory work completed on time; they have advanced notice. All the poems are classics, and I try to match them with the holidays of that particular month.

I have had students who for a religious reason could not memorize certain poems. Since I give the parents the contracts so early in the school year to review, they can easily let me know in advance if a selection is not appropriate for their child. Of course, this is not a problem for me. I simply ask the parent to submit to me a memory selection of **their** choice comparable to the one I chose for the class. I am often surprised to find that parents will choose work more difficult than I have selected for the children. Also, I will help with the selection if asked by the parent.

In this day and age, we as teachers must work very hard at keeping everyone safe and happy. Do not let this discourage you from doing things with your students. Work with your parents. You will find they **want** their children to participate in activities, and with accommodations, everyone can be safe and happy. Simply, what I am saying is, **do not use differences as an excuse to do nothing.** Also, along this same line, all of our new laws are for protecting the students and their rights; this is important, and this is good. No one wants us to stop doing activities with the children; we just need to be creative and use permission, caution, and common sense. Granted, though, it has given us as teachers more responsibility.

All students are required to do their memory work. All students must stand in front of the class to recite. Even my students who are struggling learners are required to memorize with modifications. I model for my class proper behavior for an audience. They learn we do not laugh and we are polite and attentive to those reciting. Yes, the students are very nervous in the beginning, but they will never learn public speaking skills unless we get them up in front of a group. The only way to overcome the fear of public speaking is to practice. We owe our students the opportunity to learn these skills.

After four paragraphs, I am sure you are wondering what my "Poetry Contract" has to do with community involvement; it is an integral part! At a moment's notice, my students are always ready to perform. They have their own personal "repertoire" on which to build a program. And we do build programs! For example, in February, we build a whole program around "The Gettysburg Address." It is like planning a meal, once I have the meat, all I have to do is add the vegetables! I know, some of you are vegans, but you get my point…

I also encourage the students to volunteer to recite in their local churches, 4H Clubs, Scouts, etc. On Mother's Day Sunday, I always have students reciting in their churches, and I do try to attend the services. One year our daughter complained that I spent more time with my students than I did with my own children on Mother's Day. So that year, Julie accompanied me to three morning church services in our small community to hear my students recite. We both still talk about that Sunday and how much we enjoyed the various services. After that, though, our son never made the mistake of complaining!

The students also perform for our school P. T. O. and our local board of education. These groups are always glad to see student participation, and the students enjoy presenting these programs. Although the memory work is required, I do not require participation in these programs due to the after school hours and the need for parent transportation. Students, with parent/guardian permission, volunteer for these programs. I could not do these activities without the support of my parents.

The most popular community involvement in which we participate is with our local senior citizens center located here in our small town. With parent permission, students may volunteer to participate in this activity. About every other month, the students and I will go to the center after school and perform a little program and then eat a free dinner with the seniors. This has proven to be the high point in being in my classroom. Besides getting to perform and eat a delicious meal, the children really enjoy getting to know the people. Parents drop their children off around 5:00 in the evening and come back for them about an hour later. Often, some of the seniors are grandparents of my students so this makes the activity really special for all.

When the students arrive at the center, I have them go around to the seniors, introduce themselves, and shake their hands. This really teaches the students poise. The students then usually sit and chat with the seniors. Prior to eating, I have the children perform a very short program. It usually includes singing, dancing, marching, and/or recitations. For example, in November we always do a salute to Veteran's Day. Before our first visit, I practice with the students shaking hands, and we review good table manners. The students know they do not have to eat everything on their plate, but I do teach them to say, "No, thank you," rather than, "I don't like it!" I tell the children it means the same thing, but the connotation is so much nicer. In fact, I also stress this for use at home!

I could not do this activity without the help and support of my parents and our community center. Friendships are formed that are wonderful for the children and the seniors. We even invite the seniors to our fifth grade reception at the end of the school year, and many do attend.

One final example of community involvement my class performs is a "Design a Stamp" for the local post office. Each spring, I have my students design a postage stamp. I have a form that I give each student with the rectangle shape of a stamp drawn on it. Students are then asked to draw and color a stamp. I recommend they use colored pencil; markers are not allowed. Under the stamp, I have drawn lines so that students may explain their design. For example, one year a girl drew a picture of a large puppy crying. She said it would be a good stamp to put on a letter to a friend who was moving to another school. It really helps for the students to explain their designs, and their reasons are very interesting. It is also a good, short, writing activity and showcases their cursive handwriting skills.

When finished, I send the stamps with parent permission, of course, to our local post office. They are beautifully displayed in a showcase by number, **never** names. The people who come into the post office vote for the number of their favorite stamp. At our fifth grade reception, our local postmistress is one of the invited presenters. She announces to the students, parents/guardians, and guests, the winners of the contest and gives the students fabulous prizes. I am as excited as the students to hear the results of the voting.

Our local postmistress tells me how much the patrons of the post office look forward to this contest each year. She says in the spring they want to know, "When are the children's stamps coming?" The winning stamps are displayed for the remainder of the summer.

Over the years, I have truly come to believe that it does, "take a community to educate a child." Even if you are like me and live in a community so small that your school has less than 130 students in grades PreK-5, take advantage of your limited resources. With your wonderful parents and your wonderful community involved, "the sky is the limit!" Trust me, if you look for the wonderful you will find it!

Now, for the police involvement! Our community does not have a police department, but I do have one within my classroom. I have what I call the "homework police." I appoint a student, or students, to monitor the amount of homework I give during any given day. (I must admit, though, I am not a "big" homework teacher.) I call these students the "homework police." The students love it! It takes a lot of nerve to tell a teacher they have assigned too much work for one evening!

Each morning, on the left corner of my chalkboard, I always write the date and under that, any assignments for the evening. This usually consists of next day tests or memory work coming due. The students put the assignments in their school-purchased planners at that time. During the course of the day, I may add to the assignment list any work that the students did not finish throughout the school day, projects that need to be completed at home, etc. If I happen to add too much to the list, or an after school activity is in the way of studying for a test, the "homework police" come to the rescue of the class. They simply say, "Stop!"

I listen to what they have to say about the assignments or what is going on after school, and I usually agree with them. In fact, I cannot remember a time I did not, "listen to the police!" I rotate the police throughout the school year so that students of all levels of ability monitor assignments. It is amazing how responsible and considerate the students can be of each other. I have had the "police" even say the assignment was not too much for them, but it may be for others. In addition, the students themselves may complain to the "police." The "police" must decide whether their complaint is legitimate. If the "police" feel it is, they will come to me on behalf of a fellow student.

I also assign the "time police" in my classroom. If I am calling spelling words too quickly, calling for assignments, projects, or memory work due too soon, etc., these "police" stop me. The "police" will explain to me why they feel more time is needed on a project. They will also monitor the classroom and note if other students are struggling to finish or if any students give them the "time-out signal." If so, the police politely give me the same "time-out signal" that is used in football. No sound is made; this quiet signal works extremely well in the classroom.

My "police" are really a help to me. I never worry about giving too much homework or pushing my class too hard. I am free to teach. I know I am constantly being watched "by the police!"

Get your families involved, your community involved, and your students involved in your teaching! It is good public relations and it teaches children to get along and be responsible for others. For ultimately, we all have the same goal: to make a success of "our dear little ducklings!"

Appendix A
The Writing Process

Some suggestions as to where I usually introduce/use the various ducklings. As you can see, I use the same duckling multiple times.

1. **Prewriting: In this stage, students begin to generate the ideas and plan for their writing. Writers consider their intended audience, as well as the topic and format of their writing.**
   This is where I prefer to do listing. If I ever do have the students use a web, I then have them make lists from the web. I always do drafting/writing from lists.

2. **Rough Draft: In this stage, students put pencil to paper and complete the first draft of their composition.**
   Indy, Spacey or Space Cadet, Comma Queen, Cap, Punky, Goody I and Goody II, The Little Match Duck

3. **Revising: Students reconsider their writing, making additions and subtractions, reorganizing their statements, and reflecting on their work with others.**
   Indy, Spacey or Space Cadet, Comma Queen, Cap, Punky, Goody I and Goody II, The Little Match Duck

4. **Editing/Proofreading: In this stage of the writing process, writers correct spelling, grammar, and formatting.**
   Indy, Spacey or Space Cadet, Comma Queen, Cap, Punky, Goody I and Goody II, The Little Match Duck, **Neat Nick**

5. **Evaluating/Publishing: In the final stage of the writing process, students evaluate the overall quality of their work. They share a final draft of their writing with others through publishing.**
   Indy, Spacey or Space Cadet, Comma Queen, Cap, Punky, Goody I and Goody II, The Little Match, Duck, **Neat Nick**

 *NOTES:*

Appendix B
Sample Permission Form

Dear Parents/Guardians,

As you know, one of my goals as a fifth grade teacher is to have as many of my students as possible become published authors. In the near future, we will begin writing short stories, essays, and poetry in hopes of becoming published.

With your permission, I would like to submit your child's work to various publishers. If your child's work is accepted for publication, the publisher will inform you (not me). The company will then ask for written permission from you to publish your child's work. At that time, they will also ask you if you would like to purchase the book in which your child's writing will appear. You do not need to purchase the book to have your child's writing published. The only cost involved to you is if you decide to purchase a book/s. Please remember, though, just submitting the work does not guarantee publication. We will just try and try again.

I have used these companies for years and they are all good. In fact, if I have had any of your other children in class, I am still using the same companies because I like and trust them.

Please sign below and return this form to me if I may submit your child's work to become a possible published author!

Mrs. Vickie Jo Milleson
Fifth Grade Teacher

I give permission for my child,_____,to have their

work submitted for possible publication.

_____   _____
Parents/Guardians   Date

NOTES:

Appendix C
Sample Parents/Guardians Letter

Dear Parents/Guardians,

The school year is off to a great start! It was nice to meet and talk with so many of you on Back to School Night. I try to call all my parents every six weeks, so if I did not talk with you that night, I will be in touch with you.

I just wanted to let you know of a few extra activities I will be doing with the class this year. These are all **strictly volunteer** and do not have anything to do with your child's grades in my classroom.

Here are some of the extra (and I hope fun and rewarding to the students) activities that I have planned for this year.

1. We will be performing little programs at our local senior center. I have been taking students there for the past eight years. Parents bring their children (parents do not stay) at 5:00 and pick them up at 6:00. We sing, recite, and eat a free meal with the seniors. (The one requirement to this activity is that the student must learn his/her memory work, poem, each month.)

2. We send what I call "community cards" throughout the school year. I buy greeting cards for the class at the local dollar stores. When a student tells me they have a relative or friend who is sick, had a new baby, death in the family, etc., we each sign our name and the student is then the "mail person" and delivers the card for us. (Any card donations, not religious in nature, are appreciated!)

3. In the spring, we will "Design a Stamp" for the Springfield Post Office. The students will all design their own stamps. The stamps will be put in the showcase in the post office. The stamps will each be given a number (no names will show) and the community will vote on their favorite stamps. The winning names will be announced by the postmistress at our reception in May. The winning stamps and the names of the winners will be on display at the post office all summer. (If you go to the Springfield Post Office now, you will see the winning stamps from May, 2010!)

Please sign the form below to let me know you received this letter, and it is permissible with you for your child to participate in these activities.

Mrs. Vickie Jo Milleson
Fifth Grade Teacher

Yes, I have read this letter and my child _____,
may participate in these activities.

_____   _____
Parent/Guardian   Date

Acknowledgments

One thing I have learned is no one truly writes a book by themselves. This certainly applies to me. My family deserves my thanks and gratitude.

This book would probably not have been a reality without the encouragement of our daughter-in-law, Emily. We are all so very proud of our reading professor. I also need to thank her husband, our son Joe, who works as an attorney, and our grandchildren, Peyton and Claire, for lending Emily to me during the writing of this book.

Our son-in-law, John A. Frazer, has been invaluable in the writing of all my books. He is our family computer expert. John "gets me out of trouble" whenever I "lose" my writing or "freeze" my computer. Trust me; you have no idea the damage I can do on a computer. John has freely given me of his time while he is working on his dissertation for his doctorate degree.

John's wife, our daughter, Julie Ann, an attorney and teacher, is another invaluable person to my writing. Her suggestions are always taken seriously by me. I must thank our little grandsons, Justin and Jackson, for also lending me their mother and daddy while writing this book.

Our daughter, Jill, is already a better teacher than her mother will ever aspire. I need to thank her for her suggestions and support during the writing of this book. I also want to thank our son-in-law, NCIS special agent, Mark A. Puffenbarger and little grandsons, Mason, Matthew, and Michael for her time.

My sister, Connie Jean Keaton, once again did my illustrations. I always tell Connie it does not matter what I write, our books will sell because of her beautiful pictures. She, along with our middle sister, Barbara Ann Carl, set high standards for me to follow as a teacher. They, in turn, followed in the footsteps of two other wonderful teachers, our mother, Helen Catherine Ansel, and our father, teacher and attorney, William H. Ansel, Jr.

My final thank you needs to go to my husband of over forty years, William J. Milleson, Sr. Before the ideas for my **Carnation** books and **Quackers** were even born, Bill had been after me to write. He keeps me grounded (which is no easy job!) and focused, and never fails after a day of writing to say those three special words all wives love to hear, "let's eat out!"

V. J. M.

I would like to thank my husband, Joe, our son, Peyton, and daughter, Claire, for their support and encouragement while I completed my contribution to this book. As usual, Joe is great at cheering me on to "get the job done," and I cannot wait to read Peyton's first piece of writing someday!

My sincere thanks to Mrs. Milleson for the amount of patience and grace that she showed as she waited for me to finish my part of this manuscript.

I have found that in an educational environment where we often adopt one commercial program after another, the best and most sound educational ideas are the ones that are developed and proven by classroom teachers. Mrs. Milleson has so much knowledge about the "nuts and bolts" of helping students to succeed. I am honored that she allowed me to be part of her sharing of these ideas with others.

E. K. M.

Biographies

Author

Vickie Jo Milleson has been a substitute and full time teacher in the Hampshire County school system of West Virginia for over thirty years. A graduate of Shepherd College, she is the fifth grade teacher at Springfield Green Spring Elementary School where she is known for her students' consistently high achievement on standardized tests. Vickie, a Hampshire County Teacher of the Year, is also the author of **Carnation, A**
Carnation Christmas, and the soon-to-be- published, **A Carnation Circus**, a series of picture books for children. She and her husband Bill, a retired corporate engineer, are the parents of three children and grandparents to six boys and one girl. They reside in Springfield, West Virginia with their toy French poodle, Pooché.

Author

Dr. Emily K. Milleson is currently an assistant professor at Frostburg State University in Frostburg, Maryland, where she teaches reading courses in the Educational Professions department. She is a graduate of West Virginia University, and holds a bachelor's degree in Multi-Disciplinary Studies, a Master's degree in Elementary Education, and a Doctorate in Curriculum and Instruction and Literacy. Emily has taught kindergarten and second
grade, and is certified in Elementary Education, Language Arts, and Reading. She has conducted numerous staff development workshops on reading and writing topics in West Virginia, Maryland, and Pennsylvania. Emily enjoys life in the country with her husband, Joe, son, Peyton, and daughter, Claire. They reside on their family farm in Springfield, West Virginia.

Illustrator

Connie Jean Keaton, an artist and a teacher, taught school for many years using her artistic talent in the elementary classrooms of West Virginia. She was married to the late Ralph C. Keaton, a former teacher, who became an insurance and real estate agent. Connie enjoys the company of her two children, Amy, an elementary school principal, and Will, an attorney, her three grandchildren and one great granddaughter. She is also the illustrator for the **Carnation** series of children's picture books.

References

Cunningham, P. & Cunningham J. (2010). *What really*

   matters in writing: Research-based practices across the

   elementary curriculum. Boston, Mass. Pearson Education Inc.

Gradwohl, J. & Schumacher, G. (1989). The relationship

   between content knowledge and topic choice in writing.

   Written Communication, 6, 181-195.

Graham, S., Harris K., & Fink, B. (2000). Is handwriting

   causally related to learning to write? Treatment of

   handwriting problems in beginning writers. *Journal of Educational*

   Psychology, 92, 620-633.